CONTRADICTIONS

IN THE

DESIGN

CONTRADICTIONS
IN THE
DESIGN

poems

Matthew Olzmann

ALICE JAMES BOOKS
Farmington, Maine

10 9 8 7 6 5 4 3 2 1

Alice James Books are published by Alice James Poetry Cooperative, Inc.,
an affiliate of the University of Maine at Farmington.

Alice James Books
114 Prescott Street
Farmington, ME 04938
www.alicejamesbooks.org

Names: Olzmann, Matthew, author.
Title: Contradictions in the design / Matthew Olzmann.
Description: Farmington, ME : Alice James Books, [2016]
Identifiers: LCCN 2016011686 (print) | LCCN 2016018428 (ebook) | ISBN
9781938584275 (softcover : acid-free paper) | ISBN 9781938584404 (eBook)
Subjects: | BISAC: POETRY / American / Asian American. | POETRY / American /
General. | FAMILY & RELATIONSHIPS / Marriage.
Classification: LCC PS3615.L96 A6 2016 (print) | LCC PS3615.L96 (ebook) | DDC
811/.6--dc23
LC record available at https://lccn.loc.gov/2016011686

Alice James Books gratefully acknowledges support from individual donors,
private foundations, the University of Maine at Farmington, and the
National Endowment for the Arts.

ART WORKS.
arts.gov

COVER PHOTOGRAPH BY JOHN CHERVINSKY
WWW.CHERVINSKY.ORG

CONTENTS ℘

꙳ II.

꙳ III.

ACKNOWLEDGMENTS ✑

Grateful acknowledgment is made to the editors of the following publications, in which these poems, or versions of them, first appeared.

B O D Y	*"Nothing Gets Through to You Jackass"*
Connotation Press: An Online Artifact	*"A Calm Eerie War* Could Also *Spell We Are a Miracle"* "Possum Drop" "The Discipline Monkey"
Crab Orchard Review	"You want to hold everything in place, but"
Drunken Boat	"The Millihelen" "Wreckage Gallery"
failbetter.com	"The Skull of a Mastodon"
Fogged Clarity	"Imaginary Shotguns" "Meditation of a Foot Soldier Nearing Medusa's Sculpture Garden" "Build, Now, a Monument"
Forklift, Ohio	"The Man Who Was Mistaken"

Hobart   "The Skull of a Unicorn"

Hyphen   "Astronomers Locate a New Planet"

Indiana Review   "I'll Forgive John Keats, but Not You"

Gulf Coast   "The Skull of an Unidentified Dinosaur"
                                "Elegy where Small Towns Are
                                    Obscured by Mountains"
                                "Contradictions in the Design"

Kenyon Review   "In the Gallery of American Violence"

Kenyon Review Online   "The Gallery of Severe Head Injuries"

Lantern Review   "The Well"
                                "The Gallery of Every Living Thing"

Mead: The Magazine   "Prayer for an Unremarkable Day"
of Literature & Libations

Muzzle   "Still Life with Heart Extracted from
                                    the Body of a Horse"

New England Review   "Replica of The Thinker"

Poetry Northwest   "The Minotaurs"
                                "Supervillains"
                                "Nate Brown is Looking for a Moose"

Qualm   "Elegy in Which I Am Unable to Travel
                                    Faster Than the Speed of Sound"

Salt Hill   "Engine in the Shape of a Tiny Metal
                                    Dog"

Sou'wester	"The Gallery of Small Innovations"
Toad	"The Raising of Lazarus"
The Texas Review	"The Department of Doubt"
Tongue	"Prayer Near a Farm by Black Mountain, North Carolina: 11:36 P.M., Early May"
Waxwing	"Consider All the Things You've Known but Now Know Differently"

"The Department of Doubt" was also printed as a broadside as part of the Vandercooked Poetry Nights series.

"Nothing Gets through to You, Jackass" also appeared in *Best of the Net 2013* (Sundress Publications).

Thank you to Tarfia Faizullah, Jamaal May, Patrick Rosal, and Ross White, whose insight and advice helped me at different times while writing these poems. Thank you to the Bread Loaf Writers' Conference and Kundiman for their generosity and support. My Asheville writing group: Melissa Crowe, Luke Hankins, Briar DeHaven, and Brian Sneeden.

Carey Salerno, Alyssa Neptune, and the staff at Alice James Books for bringing this book into the world.

Cathy Linh Che for reading an earlier version of this manuscript.

And Vievee Francis for being the first reader for every poem in this book.

—For Kurt and Mary Ann Olzmann

I went to the museum where they had all the heads and arms from the statues that are in all the other museums.

—STEVEN WRIGHT

When man wanted to make a machine that would walk he created the wheel, which does not resemble a leg.

—GUILLAUME APOLLINAIRE

REPLICA OF *THE THINKER*

By the doorstep of the museum,
the Duplicate is frustrated.
Like the offspring of a rock star or senator,
no matter what he does, it's never enough.
He only wants to think dignified thoughts,
important thoughts, thoughts that will imprint
like an artist's signature on the memory of mankind.
But it's difficult, because when he thinks,
his head is filled with iron and bronze,
not neurons and God.

I, too, feel like that.
You know how it works when you make a photocopy
of a photocopy? The eye fights to see the original,
which appears blurred in each new version.
Each morning, I sit at the kitchen table
the way my father must've years ago.
I've got my oatmeal and coffee,
my newspaper and blank stare.
                                        The Replica

digs his right elbow into his left thigh,
his chin into his right fist, and then he thinks
as hard as his maker will allow. He tries to envision
patterns among celestial bodies, the mysteries
of Christ, X + Y, crossword puzzles, free will.
The expression on his face:
somewhere between agony and falling asleep.

Yet he holds this pose
as if no one will notice what frauds we are,
as if some world around him is about to make sense,
some answer has almost arrived. Almost.

I. ∽

BUILD, NOW, A MONUMENT

No longer satisfied by the way time slips
through his life's work, the maker
of hourglasses yearns for a change.

He elects to construct a staircase instead.
Rather than grains of sand,
he'll manufacture one stair after another
to lament every transient second.

Look at it now! It rockets upward, almost vertical,
beginning in his backyard, puncturing
the cloud cover, and everyone speculates
where it will end. It will end
where all ambitions end: in the ether,
where the body ceases and a story continues.

But for now, it's a monument.
For now: a defiance, misoneism.
A bridge between
Earth and what Earth cannot touch.

What does he think as he builds?
Mostly he contemplates the work:
the sawdust, the anger, the hammer.
But sometimes he dreams of cars, highways,
of crashes and sequestered wreckage.
Old pain. He had a friend, out there.
There was a highway, a vehicle overturned.

If his friend was here today,
she'd understand this monument.
She liked the sky, country music, and caterpillars.

There are four thousand muscles in a caterpillar.
It uses every one of them
to become something other than itself.
Is the body a cocoon? the man wonders.

From the top of the staircase, the life
he left below is almost unrecognizable.
Look at the beagle, yelping in the neighbor's yard.
The rooftops of the shrinking houses. Everything
getting smaller as his view of the world

expands. The roads marked by petite yellow lines.
Graceland and Grant's Tomb and whatever's left
of the Parthenon. All of it is down there.
Things end. But what he can't comprehend
is how, around those endings, everything else
continues.

CONSIDER ALL THE THINGS YOU'VE KNOWN
BUT NOW KNOW DIFFERENTLY

—*After Steve Orlen*

In Michigan, on his seventh birthday,
a boy is given an old toolbox. *Thank you,*
he says, for the toolbox, *Thank you,*
for the wrench dotted with rust,
Thank you, for the greased screwdrivers,
and the needle-nose pliers. Just imagine
all the wonders the boy can build
or repair now, right? No siree!
Immediately, he sets out to discover
how the world was made
by unmaking everything the world has made.

A light falls from its fixture, and he says, *Thank you.*
A fence, relieved of its nails, and he says, *Thank you.*
Sudden three-legged chairs. Bookshelves
spilling their belongings to the floorboards.
Thank you, he says. *Thank you.* A demolition man?
Not really. Better to call him "curious,"
one who looks, then understands,
how everything secedes, returns to dust.
Items currently damaged are held as a counterpoise
to the items inevitably (but not yet) damaged.

There used to be elves in the forest beyond our houses.
Green men and blind angels.
A barefooted prophet stepping out onto the waves
of moss. There's nothing that can't be explained.
Look at the boy as he looks out at the field.
And now the field is gone.

So why then does he keep saying, *Thank you*?
And when will he stop? Only time will tell.
Or maybe we should say: only time would have told,
as the child has taken that apart as well.
Piece by ancient piece. Bone, hair, hinges.
Father Time, like an antique watch.
Little screws missing. Revelations everywhere.

IN THE GALLERY OF AMERICAN VIOLENCE

the musket sulks in the corner.
Not only is it exhausted, it feels
utterly humiliated. A pack of wild
school kids huddles around
the display case, bored,
terribly skeptical that this device—
with its smoothbore barrel
and cherrywood stock—could have ever
punched a hole in a bewildered soldier.
They scribble a few notes then dash off
to some flashier exhibit:
an early land mine perhaps,
or a car window used in a modern drive-by.
How lonely the musket feels, forgotten
in its glass prison, dust on its muzzle,
dust in its mouth. Send me back to the end
of the eighteenth century, it thinks.
There, it stalked the battlefields,
a God without mercy. Blood on the blades
of grass, blood on its bayonet,
a hungry tooth. A celebration
thunder-stomping its way through the smoke.
Cannon songs. Banners waving in the dark.
There were fewer stars, it thinks, on the flag
back then, but more in the sky.

THE MILLIHELEN

Unit for measuring beauty. One millihelen is the amount of beauty
that will launch exactly one ship.

—URBANDICTIONARY.COM

Everyone knows about the beauty that launches
a thousand ships. Her hair unfurls like a flag
and the navy, inflamed, will follow that flag until
everyone is dead. There is power in that. We know.

But what do we know about the power of the other,
the one that launches *exactly one ship?*
And what do we know of that one ship? It goes without
kettledrums or cannon fire, without Achilles or Odysseus,
without the blessings of the Gods, or even their scorn.
No one notices. No epic poem will boast of its bravery;
in fact, as it sails from the choked harbor, it sails
straight out of history and into a night so unknowable,
not even the blind eyes of Homer can guess where it will land.

It would have been easier to stay with the fleet.
There's confidence in numbers. Consider the armada
of stars as they burn heaven above us,
so certain as they scorch their way through infinity.
Why should they bother to track a single vessel
among all the waves? I'll tell you.

In the story that launches a thousand ships, beauty
is a destination, something to crash toward.
In the story that launches only one, there is no destination.

Beauty was there, among the wharves, with her
simple scarves at the beginning.
A sailor and his joy stepped from the pier and into
the fragile boat together. Why was there only one?
Because you, dear, said to the night, *I don't care
about the rest.* And I said, *Neither do I.*
And then the harbor was behind us.

THE MINOTAURS

*Please someone go upstairs and check
to see if the people who live above me
are or are not Minotaurs . . .*

—MIKE SCALISE

1.

The TV set: smashed.
Three of the four front windows: smashed.
The medicine cabinet: mauled beyond recognition.

Upstairs, the neighbors play like natural disasters.
They don't mean to keep you up all night.
It's just that their apartment is too small for their bodies
and they have nowhere else to go.

Other objects that met their demise: one record player,
one full-length mirror, two nightstands,
one Tivoli glass cabinet and all eighteen pieces
of the Royal Albert Old Country Roses tea set it once held inside.

The curtains: drawn up tightly, even in the day.
The groceries: purchased by a courier and delivered long after dark.

2.

In my apartment, I stare at the ceiling. The people upstairs
laugh like the drinkers of vodka, crash like bowling pins,
trains that have forgotten the meaning of their tracks.

They don't sound angry, only loud.
Just two people singing and stomping and shoving
over the bookcases night after night.

I could call the cops,
but I remember this past summer,
when the last couple who lived there was evicted.

I never saw them, not even in passing.
Just came home one day and their belongings
were piled out front: a labyrinth
of end tables, chairs made of oak, coatracks,
trinkets and curiosities.
A dining table with teeth marks on its surface.
A grandfather clock with its face ripped off and its guts torn out.

IMAGINARY SHOTGUNS

—Jordan Davis and many others

There's a teenager in an SUV, shopping mall, or nightclub
with an imaginary shotgun. The weapon belongs to him,

but he doesn't—he can't—know it's there. That's one problem
with an imaginary shotgun: if one is unaware of its existence,

one might feel safe enough to forget about the possibilities,
to hope the night sky is glorious and the birds

are really singing. It's late and as the streetlights begin
to buzz, one might hear: *You are safe.* I said:

there's a kid with an imaginary shotgun,
and the men who claim to see it will return with real guns.

Think of belief as a type of flag. You plant it in the soil
of some uncharted territory, and it tells everyone who you are.

Suddenly, there are dirt roads around the flag. Little houses.
Then a city. Flags soaring in the breeze. This country.

You've made a choice; you have staked this as your own.
There are many lies one can choose to believe.

Say it another way: the men who claim they saw a shotgun,
haven't seen anything. They have planted a flag, and will give

nothing back. What, exactly, do they believe?
They believe that they will be believed.

Many times I have chosen to believe in the good of all men,
Providence, the road from here and where it goes.

I have been terribly wrong.

STILL LIFE WITH HEART EXTRACTED
FROM THE BODY OF A HORSE

Question: what has two heads, yellow teeth,
and eyes made of grape jelly?

What has green stripes, nostrils that flare like caves,
and a tail that dissolves like a braid of smoke?

At the community center in the center
of Detroit, the kids draw the strangest horses.

The greatest racehorse of all time was Secretariat.

We don't see horses like Secretariat in Detroit,
so if one kid imagines a stallion that gallops through McDonald's,
and another has purple wheels instead of legs,
no one asks any questions.

When Secretariat ran a race, he usually won.

The horses the kids make, here, are different.
Some have manes that whip
like flags or confetti or streamers in the breeze.
Others look more like deformed dogs.
Every single horse is running.

Secretariat ran like no other horse. The Derby,
the Belmont, the Preakness—all of them saw
this horse explode across the finish line
far in front of his rivals. Applause. Lonelier than God.

Aaron says his horse runs from the devil.
And Tania says her horse runs from the prince.

Their teacher tells me, for Aaron, the devil is a city of rust,
a house empty and charred and tasting like gasoline.

For Tania, the prince is a father whose temper
rumbles like trains in those old movies—it barrels through
the dark, unstoppable, and everyone

knows the tracks ahead are splintered, and everyone
knows the sound of the wreck.

Jason says his horse runs from an ambulance siren
that sings its song a little closer every night.

Dana says her horse runs straight to heaven

to be with her brother: his body
no longer a doorway opened by the heel of a boot.

I'm a guest in this classroom and feel like a tourist
in a country where all the postcards are made of pain.

They ask me if I have any poems about horses.

I don't.

So I just tell a story of a horse
that ran until it was no longer a horse.

Then one child hands me her drawing.
Around it, she's made a massive heart,
and this makes sense because winning jockeys
always talk about how much heart their horses have.

How can you measure heart?

I have never seen this much ache in a single room.
After the class has ended, the teacher pins
each drawing to the board.

She is so careful, her hands shake.

"When they come back," she says, "I want them to feel
like they've built a museum,
like they've accomplished something amazing."

On the day Secretariat died, they cut his body apart.
When his heart was removed,
it should have been comparable to a small melon;
it should have weighed six to seven pounds.
It was over three times that size.

POSSUM DROP

New Year's Eve
Brasstown, North Carolina

Around here, they don't flaunt a glitter-flushed
disco ball over the town square. At midnight,
they drop a possum. You heard me:
I said, *Possum*. Welcome to North Carolina.
Happy New Year. May your next year outshine
the year of the possum, who was having
a fine year—an anxious and shy year, yes,
but otherwise fine—until he was chosen.
In the name of tradition, entertainment, or superstition,
the well-meaning of our civilization will do
freaked-out things. I submit as evidence the launch
of any new year, like the launch of a cruise ship:
as it leaves the port on its inaugural voyage,
the noise must be extravagant.
In Romania, they wear bear costumes.
In Johannesburg, South Africa, furniture is flung
from windows. Scarecrows burn in Ecuador,
and there's a village in Peru where fistfights settle
the year's grudges. But in Brasstown, North Carolina,
they drop a possum. One nervous marsupial, plucked
from the pines, imprisoned in glass, and dangled above
a mob scene of beer cans and black powder muskets,
then dropped, or *gracefully lowered* if you believe
the spectators, or believe there's anything graceful
about frightening the already frightened.

Here's another story. Instead of a possum,
picture a lion. Rome. The Coliseum.
On one side: a convicted man.

On the other: an appetite, endless teeth.
Everyone knows who will win this contest,
but in the rarest of games, the clamor of the crowd
becomes so intense, the lion startles,
backs away, too scared to attack.

Can you see it?
The captive with a stone in his hand: terrified.
The muscled predator, all claw and fang: terrified.
Do you recognize the story yet? Always, that fear
in the circle. Always, that crowd: poised, ready.

THE SKULL OF AN UNIDENTIFIED DINOSAUR

does not belong to the dinosaur skeleton
to which it has been attached.
A man thought he made an amazing
discovery. Now, it's a towering mistake,
one for which he'll likely lose his job,
but only after taking this skyscraper
of bones—with its eye sockets
like windows to hell—apart.
Femur by mandible, I know what it means
to watch your good fortune change its mind.
Like that time in college, when my friend's
supermodel cousin invited us to a party
and accidentally kissed me in the dark.
She thought I was someone else—I have
no idea *who*—but the gist of the story
can be seen in her freaking out
when the light ruined everything.
For a moment, I thought I discovered
a new world. And what a world it was—
with its beaches of untouched skin
and its moons that smelled of a hundred flowers.
I named that land *I-Could-Live-Here-
Forever Land* and *Holy-Shit-Was-I-Wrong Land.*
Einstein says imagination is more important
than knowledge. Certainly, it's kinder.
I imagine the man who wired these
dinosaur bones must have imagined
his vision was real, must have pictured
it alive. Covered in flesh, the imagined life
can also be terrifying—able to cleave you
open with the swipe of a claw
or devour you in seconds.

But as it is now, having never existed
after tricking you into believing,
it eats at you more slowly, lets you feel
every new rip in your gut, makes you beg:
What kind of animal is this?
I call it: *The Motherfuckerasaurus.*
And, technically, that's not the right name,
but neither is the word stamped here now—
in block letters, on a bronze plaque,
screwed to the floor.

THE MAN WHO WAS MISTAKEN

No, I'm not the Associate Dean for Faculty: Teaching and Learning,
You're thinking of Gary Hawkins, is what I told
the second student this week who thought I was Gary.

Gary: who, like me, is bald and wears glasses.
Gary: who once, ten years ago, was mistaken for Moby.

Moby: who, like me, is bald and wears glasses.
I am not Moby. I am the man who was mistaken

for the man who was mistaken
for Moby. I'm okay with this distinction.

I am not Jesus. But in 1996, I shared an apartment with a guy
who would go to parties in Detroit and dance until his ankles bled.

He came home once, talking
not about Moby, but "the idea" of Moby.

I was trying to play a video game (*Street Fighter,* I think)
and was about to win the thing,

which is when he said, *You know that part*
in "First Cool Hive" where the music stops being music
and starts being tongues of fire descending across the land?

Which is when I said, *No.*

Which is when he said, *Stop being cynical.*
I'm trying to say I had a spiritual experience.
That the spirit was inside the music. I'm talking about Jesus.

Which is when I said, *Wait. You think Moby is actually Jesus?*
Which is when he said, *I think we all are.*

Which is when my guy on the TV screen
got his head kicked in and died. The game was over.

I didn't know what he was talking about. But,
looking back, I realize that music and the spirit
are fused, like that point on the horizon

where you can't tell the earth from the sky from
the smokestacks that ignite them both.

Am I saying that one face in the crowd could be any other face?
Am I saying we're not that different?
Am I saying we're all connected?

No. I'm saying my roommate ate a lot of drugs
and would come home and say crazy shit.

Once he thought our furnace was talking to him.

Which is when I said, *Why don't you tell me
what the furnace was trying to say?*

Which is when he said, *It said
that me and it would always be enemies.*

Which is when I said, *Son, that's a fight you can never win.*

Which is when he said, *Okay,* and then went
outside to dance on the hood of his car.

Which is when the cops came.

Perhaps he was right. Jesus *was* inside the music.

And that music was inside my roommate.
And the state could not tolerate it.

So they sent their troopers to make him stop.

What did the music tell him?
It told him the world was on fire.

He danced anyway.

So many people in the world.
When they dance inside the pulse of smoke
machines and strobe lights, I can't tell one
from the next from the next.

There's a word for the fear of being unable
to distinguish yourself in a place like this.

I am not Jesus. I am not Moby.
I am not Gary Hawkins.

I'm the guy who looks like that other guy—*Him*—
the one who has changed,
the one who could be someone else.

SUPERVILLAINS

The New Face of Evil dreamed it was an eagle
ripping the lungs from a sparrow,
or it was an altar for human sacrifice,
or it was seated at the head of a long table
in a boardroom six hundred feet above the metropolis,
and when it woke up, it set forth to make believers of the
    uncertain.

It sent its fists into the world to preach a gospel
of broken noses and evaporated pensions
to all who needed conversion.

Jawbone of the weak, rib cage of the frightened—
pay me what I am owed, it said. Everyone paid.

I was there in the beginning.
I don't like to talk about this.

Back then, The New Face of Evil was young and ambitious,
and even had a name: Jason or Alex or Something Like That.

Anyway, Jason or Alex or Something Like That
laid siege to a small village and set all the crops aflame,
or he maybe he was still a teenager
and cornered some poor kid in the school locker room.
Perhaps it was even earlier: he was nothing more than an angry
    child
kicking a dog in his parents' basement,
while I—also a child—stood by: terrified.

No. That's not the beginning.
It began like this.
In grade school, he was my only friend.

He studied all the time, as if he were born on a blackboard.
As if—on that blackboard—his father were made of chalk,
his mother an equation that could never be solved.
Childhood was the scrape of the eraser across that slate,
the way it kept taking everything back,
leaving him with nothing.

On the day report cards were mailed home,
I walked to his house. His father whipped him with a wire
    hanger.
I went back home. My friend went up to his room to study.
I don't know what happened next.

CONTRADICTIONS IN THE DESIGN

Here is the planet where Beethoven was deaf,
where Walt Whitman was fired for his poems.
The designer of the Eiffel Tower was afraid of heights,

and the guillotine was given the name of a man
who opposed the death penalty. And none of this
makes sense; none of this is reasonable. But this is how

the blueprint gets approved. A collection of scraggy lines,
like those illusions: posters where if you stare long enough
you'll swear an image pushes through. Don't believe it.

That's just your eyes as they begin to fail. I think of these
lapses in reason, of these men who built things,
and of what exactly they built, and of what exactly built them,

and I wonder about it all each time I envision the carpenter
who pulled this all together, the first designer who designed
Earth and all its rooms. All his fears. All his strange

quirks and bewilderments. Desires—terrifying or harmless—
scuttled like mice through his study as he studied.
How he was alone in the frost before time began.

Drafting and erasing and already: so tired, so frazzled,
confused. The tools he used, scattered about his desk.
The ripsaw, the bucksaw, the hacksaw, and the lathe.

THE DISCIPLINE MONKEY

Today, four men—disguised as medieval knights—
robbed a renaissance festival.

≥

At first, onlookers must have thought it was all
part of the show, even when one of the knights
smashed an axe handle into the face
of a festival organizer, even when the blood looked real.

≥

The crowd must have figured,
at any moment, the King and all his men
would appear, as if by magic.

≥

Any moment now,

≥

Even when the body on the ground kept bleeding.

The King must be on his way to save his kingdom.

⁂

What is a kingdom?

⁂

For the past couple days, I've been cat-sitting
for my friends Justin and Erin.

⁂

Justin told me that the cats like to play with an old shoestring.

⁂

*You drag it across the floor, and they think it's a copperhead
and try to kill it.*

⁂

But when I try this, the cats just yawn
and look bored.

&

I call Justin, and he says, *You tell those bastards
if they don't play with the snake, Daddy will come home
and release the Discipline Monkey.*

&

They'll know what that means, he says.

&

I have no idea what that means.

&

I pass the message along, and immediately feel silly
for talking to two cats about a Discipline Monkey.

&

This is not the strangest thing I've done in my life,
and I'm sure I'd feel much worse if I dressed up as a feudal lord
or a wizard and pretended to be important,
only to be rendered helpless as renegade knights
bludgeoned the serfs and robbed the vassals.

*

And that feeling would intensify,
if no royalty rode in on horseback.

*

This is how the Greeks must have felt
the day Mount Olympus became just another mountain.

*

So much stone under so much sky and no one left
to throw sparks from above.

*

I imagine a Discipline Monkey could be a chimpanzee
who has trained for years to repress his most basic urges.

*

He can sit still for hours, stack blocks on top of each other
and, if he wanted to, he could evolve, walk upright, feel empathy,
donate a kidney and save someone's life.

*

If he wanted to, he could curl his fingers around a flanged mace
and leave a world in ruin.

*

We are capable of so much good and terrible.

*

I tell Justin and Erin's cats
that a monkey can put on the clothes
of another monkey and pretend he is someone else.

*

I want to believe they're listening, but who can tell?

*

But I want to believe, and Charles Darwin once said,
Let each man hope and believe what he can.

⁓

Is this the thing that sets us apart?

⁓

The ability to hope and believe there is a King
even if that King is invisible, or wearing a costume,
or in hiding and unwilling to be found?

II.

YOU WANT TO HOLD EVERYTHING
IN PLACE, BUT

you can't hold it all. You can't keep
time from crumbling, or everyone alive just by
holding your breath. You can't stop sleep

from covering the faces of your friends. Cheap
motels, blood in the sink, nail clippings and hair dye—
you can't hold it all. You can't keep

the continents from shifting, or the deep
wells of memory from going dry.
Hold your breath. You can't stop sleep

from erasing another day. The cold sweep
of moonlight. Photographs. Your lover's thigh.
You can't hold it all. You can't keep

your hair from the drainpipe, or the beep
of the alarm clock from telling another lie.
Holding your breath can't stop sleep

from burying this year and the next beneath a heap
of fresh earth. These sparrows. This white sky.
You can't hold it all. You can't keep
holding your breath, but can't stop until you sleep.

I'LL FORGIVE JOHN KEATS, BUT NOT YOU

People talk about beauty
like a shackle made of silver,
like everyone longs for it
to lash their bodies to the earth.

Have you ever seen those little boxes,
covered in glass, where they display
dead insects? Usually it's just one.
Usually they're framed. Like pieces of art.

Beauty, like something pinned to a piece of cork,
like a blood vessel leaking its secrets,
like a fingernail that hangs
from the skin and begs you to touch it.

Let me tell you about a conversation I overheard
at a museum in California.

There was this artist boy trying to impress this artist girl
by telling her about someone from his past.
I called her "Monet," he said, *even though her name wasn't Monet.*
Because she was like an impressionist painting: beautiful

from a distance but blotchy
and fucked-up looking when you get this close.

Talking about beauty: like embalming fluid
to preserve the vehicle forever
even if the vehicle can't be preserved
and there's no such thing as forever.

Apparently, this girl was unmoved

by her suitor's obvious charms.
A change in tactics was needed.
You know, he said, *Keats once said, "A thing of beauty*
is a joy forever: its loveliness increases; it will never pass into nothingness."
Then he said, *I think about this when I look at you.*

Let me tell you about the time
John Keats was almost ruined for me forever.

And that's when Art-School-Boy noticed
I was listening. *Can I help you, friend?* he said.

Thing is, he reminds me
of just about everyone I know: all
the artists and poets, all the part-time philosophers
and their legions of followers, everyone:

all talking about the same narrow bridge.

I've seen that bridge. It's made of rope. Its edges
are frayed and it trembles in the wind.
If you try to cross, don't look down.
I know a man who has been called ugly.
I know a woman who has been called worse.

Did I mention: in this museum, there's an exhibit
of insects, their wings splayed beneath glass,
and all of this is said to be beautiful.

Yesterday, a kid jumped off a bridge
two blocks from my house.
And everyone keeps talk about pretty things.

Goddamn, you are
beautiful, a display case to marvel over.

Can I help you friend? he said, *Can I help you friend?*

Was I staring? Did I have no words?

People talk about beauty but don't define it.
As if we've all decided what it is.

As if we all agree. We do not agree.

There is the object beneath the glass
and there is the world seen
by the subject looking out from that glass.
What does this mean?

It means when I speak of beauty and you speak
of beauty, we are not speaking
about the same thing. And we are not friends.

ASTRONOMERS LOCATE A NEW PLANET

Because it is so dense, scientists calculate the carbon must be crystalline,
so a large part of this strange world will effectively be diamond.

—*Reuters, 8/25/2011*

Like the universe's largest engagement ring, it twirls
and sparkles its way through infinity.
The citizens of the new world know about luxury.
They can live for a thousand years.
Their hearts are little clocks
with silver pendulums pulsing inside.
Eyes like onyx, teeth like pearl.
But it's not always easy. They know hunger.
They starve. A field made of diamond
is impossible to plow; shovels crumble and fold
like paper animals. So frequent is famine,
that when two people get married,
one gives the other a locket filled with dirt.
That's the rare thing, the treasured thing, there.
It takes decades to save for,
but the ground beneath them glows,
and people find a way.

On Earth, when my wife is sleeping,
I like to look out at the sky.
I like to watch TV shows about supernovas,
and contemplate things that are endless
like the heavens and, maybe, love.
I can drink coffee and eat apples whenever I want.
Things grow everywhere, and so much is possible,
but on the news tonight: a debate about who
can love each other forever and who cannot.

There was a time when it would've been illegal
for my wife to be my wife. Her skin,
my household of privilege. Sometimes,
I wish I could move to another planet.
Sometimes, I wonder what worlds are out there.
I turn off the TV because the news rarely makes
the right decision on its own. But even as the room
goes blacker than the gaps between galaxies,
I can hear the echoes: who is allowed to hold
the ones they wish to hold, who can reach
into the night, who can press his or her
own ear against another's chest and listen
to a heartbeat telling stories in the dark.

A CALM EERIE WAR COULD ALSO SPELL
WE ARE A MIRACLE

Waltz, Month, Amen—
words to the strangest prayer ever said.
Also: an anagram for *Matthew Olzmann,*
just as *beep forth ethos*
contains all the letters of *hope for the best.*

You can try to do both: beep forth ethos
and hope for the best, but I've found
the former is easier than the latter.

My mom says the order of things is critical.
Cooking, for example, is not about ingredients,
but the order of specific actions combined
with the order of ingredients.

History is complicated like that: a recipe.
To have us standing here, there had to be
millions of people before us. Before that,
an animal had to drag itself from the depths.
So there needed to be a sea. Waves.
Sunlight and carbon. Let there be light, etcetera.
Clouds of gasses, swirling in the blackness
like a shot of cream in the galaxy's coffee cup.
At some point there needed to be gravity.
Let's not discount gravity. All of this heated
to a boiling point and left on the stove until now.

So many things could have gone wrong.
It's astounding that that the world exists.
It's remarkable that we exist inside that world.

Meanwhile, my father, an engineer,
puts labels on everything. The basement storage room
is airtight and alphabetized.
Try telling him order doesn't matter.
Try telling a man like that there's not a reason for everything.

Scientists once believed that the expansion of the universe
was slowing down. They were wrong. Everything
speeds up. Everything grows faster and faster apart.

Sometimes you hear the sound of brakes and know
the shriek of glass and sirens will follow.
Because *brakes* then *glass* then *sirens* is the order of a crash.
Just like grapes, sugar, yeast and fifteen months
of darkness is the order of champagne.

And a cluster of energy, followed by voice that rips
the nothingness, followed by a bang, a flash
that goes on forever, is the beginning

of the alphabet. One letter tumbles
after another and if you get them right,
you can say: *Astonishment.* Put it together
a little differently and you have the *Insanest Moth.*

Even that moth contains its own cosmos of chance
and possibility. Consider the black witch moth.
There are parts of Mexico where it's believed to be
a harbinger of death. But if it lands
on your door in Texas or the Bahamas,
you might win the lottery; you might be rich.

DELIVER US

To save us from the bullet, the Kevlar must absorb
the whistle of a copperplated projectile
at fourteen hundred feet per second.

To save us from the rogue wave
and the capsized ship, the life raft must slip past
the bull sharks and outwit the ocean on our behalf.

And no one remembers the exit sign: the light
who ushers the crowd from the smoldering room.
All that panic, all those ashes, and still
it holds steady with its hushed red voice: *This way please.*

I've watched too many movies about apocalypses.
The thing that saves us is always consumed
by the thing it saves us from.

The animal, for example, delivers us
from the question of our hunger by answering
the question of our hunger.

At the small mountain college where I work,
I walk down by the farm in the evenings.

On the farm, night comes for the cattle,
like a postman over the ridge. He's dressed in blue
with a satchel slung from his shoulder.

Then night approaches the pigs.
He is a nurse in the infirmary
with a needle of mercy.

Then night comes for the lamb.
His eyes shine like the shears.
Look how dark it gets out here.
There is no lamb.

THE RAISING OF LAZARUS

Caravaggio
Oil on Canvas
380 cm x 275 cm

To me, he still looks dead: Lazarus, fallen,
limbs rigid like planks of broken balsa wood,
resting cold, like a dead man,
in the hold of another's arms, head bent back,
as if unable to support itself, or maybe

just dead, with Jesus still pointing,
cautiously, as if to say, *Okay guys: let's try this again,*
the dark edges collapsing around the crowd
as if neither the power of Christ nor the power
of Caravaggio could change this moment.

In fact, if Caravaggio hadn't titled this *The Raising*
of Lazarus, I'd have no reason to think I was witness
to the impossible. Yet here I am, like those painted
into the crowd, watching the body for a flicker of life.
The flare of a lung. A tremble in the lips.

Here's the power of saying something, of suggestion,
where the suggestion—in this case, the painting's title—
makes the audience strain to see
what they're supposed to see: resurrection. In this way,
the title is an invocation of sorts, though my mother
used to say, *Saying something doesn't make it true.*

I have said all kinds of things that were never true.
Though I wanted them to be true, longed
for them to manifest, just as those

in this corridor long for Lazarus to rise.
Tell me: who hasn't been there among them—

who hasn't stood above a body:
a friend or parent, a cousin or brother. A room
with dead flowers and walls like the stone interior
of an ancient tomb, and who hasn't bent above that body
to plead: *No,* or *Please come back,* or *You can't be dead.*

Then the hours of watching.
Then the still life before you, as it remains still.

ELEGY WHERE SMALL TOWNS
ARE OBSCURED BY MOUNTAINS

I get news of an old friend's suicide
while I'm on the highway, in the middle
of moving from one state to another. Questions
race by me like oncoming traffic: *God,*

and *Why?* and *When?* and *How?* and then,
more difficult, one that won't become words,
like a door where the hinge jams, like a silhouette
that won't step into the light, and abruptly

I remember my dad—decades ago—wrestling
a riverbank with a fishing pole, how he struggled
with a shadow that thrashed beneath the surface
and he could never wrench it closer. The hooked

mouth chose to remain submerged and violent
below the reeds and river moss. Whatever
question I can't ask now, is like that,
but I suspect it wants to know how the world

is different today, even though it's just one person smaller
and everything looks the same. Look at the rush
of cornfields. Look at the exit signs on sheets of steel.
Watch the cities as they shrink behind us.

I had not spoken to my friend in years.
There are reasons for that, but they seem small
when the Blue Ridge Mountains surge before you.
Then, you're among those peaks. Nothing but

trees, ridges, and valleys so vast and ancient,
you suppose—if you could climb down inside one—
you'd locate the origins of Earth. Eden. Actually,
there are clusters of homes. Diners that close

at dusk. Gas stations with one pump. I hope
the afterlife is like one country road
after another, unseen from the highway,
passing through small towns the way

autumn passes through the wind chimes slung
above the front porches out here.
Look at the peeling paint, the stoic
railings, and the wood warped by rain.

There are all kinds of stories eaten by history
and silence and neglect. Above the door of a house
in the distance, something stirs the chimes and reminds
someone inside that where there is wind: a song,

however faint. A man hears it and passes
through a screen door into a night of fireflies.
He looks around as if called by a voice.
The wind has passed. The chimes are quiet.

IN THE GALLERY OF SEVERE HEAD INJURIES

My kid brother is still in college, caring
for a man who tried to kill himself
with a power drill. The task
that has been entrusted to my brother
is simple: *Make sure the tube*
in this guy's throat doesn't pop out.
So he sits there, bedside, reading
into the night. And instead of stars,
the air is possessed by pinpricks
of green light, skittering across a black
monitor, as if the monitor
were a deep field and the lights
were towheaded children playing
long after dark. And instead of crickets,
there's the rasp of a dead man's chest
that somehow still shudders up and down,
a heavy sound as if, inside, a smaller man
drags an iron reliquary across a hardwood floor.
What do you call this world, the images
that haunt the unconscious body? There,
in the hollow, perhaps the smaller man lets
go of the container, stands erect, turns
to let the sun touch his ruined face.
His loved ones rush toward him.
Birds flicker over everything. Some would say
this is a dream. This is nothing like a dream.

THE GALLERY OF SMALL INNOVATIONS

A young man is given a cube.
You know the one: it's made of several
smaller blocks, connected
by a joint that twists in any direction.
He studies the squares, then twists them.
Soon, he can't return the squares
to their original positions.
What we have now, is a puzzle.
What we have now, is only one solution.
He twists. He is older. The solution
seems unattainable. He shows the puzzle
to his friends. And he is older again.
His parents make their exits. First,
his mother falls apart and is lost
in the maze of her mind. Then, his father
disappears forever through a trapdoor
in an aortic valve. And the man keeps
twisting the cube. Still no solution.
By now, he doubts one actually exists.
The firm where he works lays everyone off.
The sun goes down. His kids are grown.
He has a cough, bad knees, and when
he shakes the puzzle, he shakes
the world itself—this place where nothing
can be fixed, nothing can be set back
to the way it was. He holds the cube
to the light, then to his ear as if listening
for a secret. If he listens hard enough,
he thinks he hears it: a sound so far off,

it's impossible to distinguish: the
murmur of friends gathered at the end
of a hallway, the splash of a single frog
into a pond surrounded by night,
or a quiver of bees so thick
around a tree that the tree can't be seen.

CREATION MYTHS

Realizing the possibility that my wife and I might never have
children, I write a brief note to that which does not exist.

I'm glad I'll never have to bail you out of jail.
I'll never have to carry you into an emergency room.
I'll never have to explain politics,
or what they're thinking in Wisconsin, or Arizona,
or even next door where one man is shouting holes
into his children and you can almost hear the fear
inside their bodies. So many things are being broken.

But I wish you could've met your mother.
She would've given you a better childhood than the one
she remembers. She makes pancakes with sour cream
and watches cartoons and sings to herself
when she's sleepy, and you would've loved her.

You would have been good at some things, and I would have
been terrible if you asked for help
with your science or math homework.
Still, I would have enjoyed telling you stories before bed.
Mostly fairy tales and stuff about dragons.

But also tales about life and the beginning of the universe.
No one is exactly sure how that happened.
Some will say, there is a God. Others will argue:
a shiver of light shattered in all directions.
But what most agree on is this: at some point
there was nothing. I cannot imagine
what nothing looks like. How cold it is, how vast
or how lonely. I don't know how matter forms.

Or how love exists. I don't know why creation
happens, and happens, and sometimes does not.
But I know this: at some point there was nothing.
Then suddenly, in the middle of all that nothing,
according to some stories at least,
there was, unexplainably, something.

WRECKAGE GALLERY

> *The world could've been anything. Instead, it was this.*
> —I'm quoting you. You said that.

After we were tourists in the land
with cell phone towers staked into the ground like hypodermic needles.

After I worked in the theater, and our money ran out, and I filled
a trash bag with stale popcorn and dragged it home for dinner.

After that night when men pushed their junk carts
of machine parts and bent umbrellas past our car that wouldn't start.

After the railroad throat, the stentorian uproar of the engine,
but no train in sight, just tracks, quiet as iron, languishing along Lake Erie.

After I worked as a telemarketer, and dialed a thousand numbers everyday,
but never heard your voice.

After the inventory of ruins: seventy thousand
crumbling buildings in Detroit alone. Among them: a furnace factory,
a cathedral, your cousin's house.

After you stayed awake in your apartment, the curtains drawn,
reading to me.

After the Midwestern blackout and the whole grid
collapsing like a bad lung. So hot no one could breathe.

No power. No gas. Vehicles left for dead, roadside.
Everyone: roasting spoiling meat in parking lots.

After I got a job as a driver, hauling tissue samples across the state,
and I went out in a storm and barely made it back.

The metal of a semitruck merges with the metal of my car.
The large machine amputates a smaller machine.

War glistens on every TV screen.
After static from the speakers, like birds choking on garbage.

After they found a giant mushroom-like fungus growing from the waste
in some abandoned warehouse, and no one knew what it was.

After the North Pole, like a hunted animal,
conceded more and more ground.

After another winter, living in Hamtramck,
and padlocks on all objects that had hinges,
and you were the only warm thing I knew.

After the spring thaw, and the alley pooled with melted snow.
After it froze again, and the bodies of rats, newly dead, perfectly
beneath the ice, as if Nature wanted them cryogenically preserved.

After the storm
that scrubbed the earth like a hazmat cleanup crew.

You're holding my arm. I'm almost
smiling at the camera, proud, as if to say:
Here is my life. The thing I didn't destroy.

After all this, you gave me the photo,
months or years later,
and I was surprised anything could last that long.

III.

THE DEPARTMENT OF DOUBT

—After Jenny Johnson

It's lonely for those who work the swing shift
in The Department of Doubt.

At a party, if you tell someone about your employer,
they'll turn and talk to someone else.

Your achievements will be ignored. Your labors:
met with a roll of the eyes.

No one ever says, *You need to doubt yourself
if you want to succeed.*

You'll never hear someone promise, *Only doubt
will get you into Heaven.*

It's *believe* this, and *faith* that,
and *trust* in this, and *yes* to that.

No one cares how hard it is, what harm comes for you:
the grindstone pinning you to your midnight desk.

Your amaranthine questions. Your armory
of test tubes and calipers. Your hole-punchers

that punch holes into doctrine
and dogma, law books, and fairy tales.

But you work late and push your stone of uncertainty—
like Sisyphus, through the night—

because you must.

It's been this way since Earth was flat.

Even then, protesters would besiege The Department.
Peek between the curtains. Are they still out there now?

Pitchforks and torches. All that belief.
All that fire getting closer.

NOTHING GETS THROUGH TO YOU, JACKASS

When Catullus says it,
it sounds more eloquent
than when I say it:
Nothing gets through to you, jackass.

When I forget
to put gas in the gas tank.
When I miss every deadline.
When I accidentally flood the kitchen.

When I buy the wrong kind of light bulbs
and everything I build goes dark
like a condemned building, and the news says
get ready for more of the same,

because everyone we know keeps
flying off this earth, and it's autumn now
so the leaves are letting go of their branches
as if they too are ready

to evacuate this town,
and one day— whether we like it or not—
we will follow, and my knuckles feel
rough and helpless,

and I want pound my face through the drywall
or heaven: nothing—not reason
or a tender voice—
nothing gets through.

Yes, there are other jackasses.
Better, more accomplished jackasses.

Cities. Countries.
Once, there was even a TV show dedicated

to men who skateboarded from the rooftops
of houses and garages, lit
themselves on fire, kicked each other
in the balls, and laughed about it.

But they've got nothing on this jackass.
They had to *try* to be that stupid.
Me? I am working my hardest, every single day,
to act like a normal person.

But I slam a door when I mean
to say I love you.
I back my car into another
when I'm trying to move forward.

NATE BROWN IS LOOKING FOR A MOOSE

Shrouded in fog, dignified and reticent: a moose.
When Ross White goes outside in Vermont,
he sees one immediately.

When Jamaal May goes outside, he sees one as well.
As if they are everywhere.

But when Nate Brown goes outside, he sees
only the absence of a moose, spaces
where one might have stood but no longer stands.

He's been hoping to see one for years.
So he practices his moose call, and nothing happens.
He stands tiptoe, on one leg,
narrows his eyes. Nothing happens.

What he has now is a mission, a quest,
a calling that can't be denied.

It's dusk and he stares into the dark. The world
is full of dogwoods and elm trees, and behind the branches,
ten thousand more—all leafy and stupid
and yielding no answers.

What do I mean? I mean
despite everything, we might search
for something and never find it.

When I was a teenager, several of my friends
suddenly found God.
I tried, but found only pocket lint and angst.

The loser of some holy scavenger hunt,
the last to cross the finish line,
kneeling in church, whispering
to heaven: *Dude, where are you?*

What made it worse was everyone's conviction.
The candles and prayer groups,
the smugness of their repeating, *Well, you know,
if you look behind you and see only one set of footprints—*

What makes Nate Brown's quest equally difficult
is how our friend Chip Cheek leans back in his chair
and says, *Oh Man—out here they grow big as dinosaurs.*

And how Kellam Ayers's eyes fill with mist
when she nods and says, *Yes, they're almost   magical.*

And so a man goes back into the fields
and tries not to move. Goes
out to the forest and tries not to move. Goes
down to the river
and pretends he's part of that river.

He is a stone, a branch, a fallen maple leaf.
He is (sort of) patient
and he'll see this thing or hold his breath forever.

I think of myself as a teenager and how
I'm no different now.

At home, my wife has a numbness, a weakness that spreads
through her body and no doctors
can figure it out. When she sleeps,

I'm afraid of everything and I pray into her hair
like I'm young again

on my knees in a church, in search of an answer.

Sometimes I go outside, and the dark is so prodigious—
the way it remedies everything by covering everything.

I like thinking of how my friend stares
down this same darkness
as if it will offer the index to some temporal secret.

What we're looking for are miracles.

Out there—
there could be nothing.

Or there could be antlers and hooves.
Lumbering mysteries.
They plod across the quiet fields.

PRAYER FOR AN UNREMARKABLE DAY

I'd like a day where all the buildings remain intact.
Let the Hydra remain asleep beneath the surface.
Let the tornado be befuddled, yawn,
go back to bed. No floods. No lightning strikes.
No movie theaters where a man walks
in with a terrible idea hidden in his coat.
Forgive me, for I have longed

for special effects, glory. Flashbulbs and moon landings.
Not anymore. Give me something ordinary, a day
that doesn't swerve into the wrong lane.
Give me commercials for hand soap,
safety goggles, Lipton tea.

In 499 B.C., back on the shores of Miletus,
Histiaeus tattooed instructions
to the shaved head of his favorite slave.
When the hair grew back, the message was sent
to a general, who took a razor to the slave,
saw the command, and began torching
the countryside, killing the weak. Always,
this is how bad news arrives.

I thought I could protect people.
Today: my brother buys a house on a fault line in California,
and my parents—like everyone else—
grow one year older, one year at a time.
But that happens faster now.
I'm not sure how it's possible, but already
one can see fissures in both
the pavement and the sky,

how the trees, branded by the storm,
lean until their roots are loosed from the land.

Let the news be boring. Let the roof repel the rain.
Let the car start on the first or second try.

ELEGY IN WHICH I'M UNABLE TO TRAVEL FASTER THAN THE SPEED OF SOUND

When I saw his body—which was no longer
his body, but something else: a replica
of his body, an artist's rendering of his
body, a replacement body, something
made of wax and hair and human tissue
and shaped to look almost identical
to the way I remember him—the air
left my lungs as if I were a balloon
and grief were a slow needle held
by an invisible hand. I don't know
where that air goes. I don't know
if it stayed in the room to be breathed
in by others, to be absorbed by their
quick blood, to be rushed through arteries,
and to later supply their brains with oxygen.
If so, what sad thoughts might they have thought
in the moment that oxygen found them?
Pain moves through the body at a rate
of three hundred fifty feet per second.
This means pain travels fast, but not as fast
as sound. This means, when someone speaks,
pain is slower than that language. If someone
would have said, *Please*, or *Help*,
those words would have made it to the other side
of the room, or through the door, before
the feeling—inside your clenched fist—
of your fingernails
drawing blood from your palm
registered in your brain. But I don't remember
anyone saying anything like that.
I don't remember anyone speaking.

ENGINE IN THE SHAPE OF A TINY METAL DOG

In one of Diego Rivera's murals, Henry
Ford lectures a group of auto workers.
Between them, an engine. From the engine,
the gear shaft grows into a tail, two disks
appear as eyes, four legs sprout from the base.
The docent points to that dog and explains:
in pre-Columbian graves, ceramic dogs
were buried to guide the spirit from one world
to the other. So too, we're told,
the engine guides us from one era to another.
Something felt off with the analogy—
when a man sits behind a wheel, he expects
to reach his destination alive. Still, I wondered
what I might be buried with when I make my exit.
What hound sleeps outside my door,
ready to lead me from a city of empty warehouses
to a clearing of river birch and moonlight?
Last week, I attended a funeral far from home.
My fear, like a coyote howl in the distance.
My hesitation, the slowing of four black tires, the rasp
of gravel underneath. Exhausted from driving
across three states, I didn't know what to say
when an usher at the church told me I needed
to try speaking to the Lord—that I should
make an appointment—as if God had an office
down the hall, a secretary to help with his calendar,
and if I just snuck around the corner,
I'd see him sitting behind a desk, working on
his taxes or grading papers as he waited
for me to drop in. But as I looked at the usher,
then the faces of the bereaved, in the middle
of a city whose roads made little sense,

there might have been an animal made of iron
on the grounds, but I couldn't summon the strength
to track it down or language to make it heel.

THE GALLERY OF EVERY LIVING THING

Consider Adam rolling through the garden, sentenced
to name the animals. Hello, frog.
Hello, wolf. Hello, marmoset and three-toed sloth.
At first: what joy! What beauty!
Hello, ring-tailed lemur.
Hello, star-nosed mole, zebra, and banana slug.
How he breezed back and forth,
between the north and south gates, pointing
and naming, codifying and organizing.
Hello, cotton rat and prairie racerunner.
Good morning, blue whale and tiger prawn.
Such musical beasts—with their trumpet throats
and xylophone scales, their accordion lungs
and kick drum muscles—he'd announce the names
and the names would sing back.
Hello, red-bellied newt.
Pleased to meet you, antelope and dragonfly.

But the work was impossible, tedious
and more exhausting by the day.
Who can notice the shift from a thing with a thousand legs
to a thing with a thousand and one?
(There's a difference, and each difference needs a name.)
Frequently, he ran out of names, and entire families
of dinosaurs slid from the globe
before he could tell them what they were.
Goodbye, triceratops. Goodbye, stegosaurus.
He was told to be more specific; he was told
to be faster and more exact. Word came down
from the boss that simply calling everything
with four legs and whiskers a "cat"

would no longer suffice: Hello, clouded leopard.
Hello, bobcat. Hello, Egyptian Mau and Kurilian Bobtail.

I can hardly imagine how he suffered.
I, who can barely keep my checking account in order,
who can hardly tell the difference
between a Tuesday and Wednesday,
between a new friend and someone
who might leave my body crumpled in an alley,
my wallet missing and my name unknown.
To know the difference between the poisonous
and the tender. To remember
the variations of every tooth and claw.

Imagine the ache in his head as he struggled to hold
his library catalogues of skins and furs,
his Audubon indexes of talons and feathers,
to hold all of this, everything, burning, in his skull.

Who wouldn't long for some kind of release?
Who wouldn't scan the landscape for an exit route,
as he, without sleep, kept pointing and naming,
pointing and naming, each time hoping
that this one was the last one?
But there is no end, he discovered.
Not even when he named the trails of ants
that latticed themselves over and under
the iron fence posts, or the worm
in the fruit, or the thing that crawled toward him,
on its belly, anonymous and kind.

THE SKULL OF A UNICORN

It "might" be a hoax.
That's what they're reporting.
"Might" be a hoax.
Not *is* a hoax.
Not *definitely*, not *obviously*,
not *clearly, certainly, undeniably,*
irrefutably, incontestably, assuredly,
or even *What are you talking about—*
of course this is a hoax.
Instead: "might" be a hoax.

Did you hear about how the word "might"
became the single, greatest word
in the English language?
It happened about fifteen seconds ago.

Might. Such a beautiful ambiguity.
The way it leaves the door open—just a smidge.
No one gets excluded.
It welcomes us all into its home: doubters,
cynics, and those who just crave
the relentless possibility
that there is something enchanted,
however tenuous, however unlikely,
buried in this land. Between
the Taco Bells and tension wires and windswept parking lots.
There is something good to be found.
It says, *Come on in. Have a seat next to me.*
Drink from my cup. Here.
Anything might happen.

THE WELL

To the well, with buckets, I go.
To the empty, to the hole, with greed, I go.
To the hand that gives, I ask for more.

The fields arch their spines until
their ribs press through the soil.

The orchard offers no more fruit, only birds,
and I pluck one from every bough.

To the stove, with my plate of birds, I go.
To the sky, with my belly howling, I go.

Let the river try to hide.
Let it burrow under the earth.
Let it sing in hidden caverns.

I will find it.
I will build a well.

THE SKULL OF A MASTODON

Covered with faint carvings, a skull is wrenched
from the earth. The symbols etched on its crown
are strange to the archaeologist
who bends above it the way a whooping crane
bends above water. The crane looks
into the ripples for a midafternoon snack.
The archaeologist looks into the skull for meaning.
The carvings could be a poem or eviction notice.
Who knows? What's certain is someone else
held this skull, someone else was here.
How long is anything here? Thomas Jefferson
believed that, here, on this earth,
there were many living mastodons, still romping
through the wild, celebrating their hairy existence
in the unexplored territories of this country.
He didn't believe in extinction.
That Thomas Jefferson is now extinct
speaks to a flaw in his theory. Search for yourself—
in shopping malls and mountain ranges
and rain forests—you'll find Thomas Jefferson
as often as a mastodon. The mastodon
is gone, out to lunch forever, retired
to realms of fog and sleep. It survived tar pits,
saber-toothed tigers, and glaciers but fell
when struck by a spear thrown from a hand.

The hand that threw the spear is not much
different from the one I use to lift the remote
to switch the History Channel to the next channel.
On the next screen, the stock market crashes.
On another, a pugilist swings and swings
as blood sloshes from his mouth. The dark

beyond my window could be the same dark
the scientist sees when he peeks into the empty
sockets of the ancient. History feels so close
right now, I can almost hear it clomping across
the plains and into the parking lot outside.
Before sleep, I press my fingers to my face
and imagine the ridges beneath.

PRAYER NEAR A FARM BY BLACK MOUNTAIN, NORTH CAROLINA: 11:36 P.M., EARLY MAY

Our Father, who art in
heaven and also
the centipede grass and the creek
and the engine that warbles
roadside: thank you
for the black
silhouette of mountains,
deep black
against the regular black
of the night. Thank you
for the field between me
and them
even though I can't see it.
And thanks for the ability to imagine
what can't be seen.
I imagine you
just as these lowing cows
must have faith in the field
as they glide across it
seeing nothing out here
but the outlines of each other,
my headlights,
an obliterated barn in the distance.

MEDITATION OF A FOOT SOLDIER NEARING MEDUSA'S SCULPTURE GARDEN

So these are the monuments.

And these are the faces of the inevitable.

And if I am made one of them, rendered

motionless, made

marble by the Gorgon's stare, then

let me celebrate the abrupt

tombstone my torso becomes.

I've never been this far from home.

I've never lifted my arms above

my head in victory as the rose petals

fell like rain. If I am never

to move again, let me never

take for granted

how I've been granted

this permanence, this patience

to stand forever—a stone

in this small corner of history—

among this statuary, able

to outlast birds, winged

horses, and their riders.

RECENT TITLES FROM ALICE JAMES BOOKS

Alice James Books has been publishing poetry since 1973. The press was founded in Boston, Massachusetts as a cooperative wherein authors performed the day-to-day undertakings of the press. This collaborative element remains viable even today, as authors who publish with the press are also invited to become members of the editorial board and participate in editorial decisions at the press. The editorial board selects manuscripts for publication via the press's annual, national competition, the Alice James Award. Alice James Books seeks to support women writers and was named for Alice James, sister to William and Henry, whose extraordinary gift for writing went unrecognized during her lifetime.

Designed by Dede Cummings
DCDESIGN

Printed in the USA
CPSIA information can be obtained
at www.ICGtesting.com
LVHW090355151123
763992LV00004B/509

9 781938 584275